MW01519010

Air Fryer Oven Cookbook

Discover healthy and crispy air fryer oven recipes with images both for beginners and advanced users

Linsdey Green

—

Table of Contents:

Introduction

Air fryers are the new and improved version of frying, healthier and faster than any way of cooking before it. Air fryers use just 30% oil to cook a variety of food, leaving the other 70% to be filled with flavor-producing moisture that would otherwise be lost in traditional deep-frying Directions. With an air fryer oven, you can easily make a whole meal without ever having to turn on the stove or oven. Utilizing an air fryer is a very simple and convenient process, but it does take some practice to learn the specifics. It requires little oil, little preparation time and produces a healthier meal. With the right air fryer oven, you can make all your favorite meals with ease in just minutes. There are different types of foods that can be cooked using an air fryer oven, including appetizers, snacks, pieces of bread, main courses and desserts. Whatever your cooking style, there is an air fryer oven out there for you.

Cooking is a science and it takes time to learn how things work. Using an air fryer for the first time might be strange at first. It may yield some time getting used to, but once you get the hang of it you may find that it is just as easy and convenient as using a conventional oven or frying pan.

Top 4 Models of the Air Fryer Oven

The best air fryer oven is the Hamilton Beach 25100 Air Fryer Oven. With this oven, there are two thermostats. One will be used to cook foods with hot air and the other one is for food that has been pre-heated in the microwave. You can choose either set to achieve what you want. The oven is compatible with all types of convection baking elements as well. It has a non-stick coating that makes it easy to clean in case of spills or food debris.

Next, the Black & Decker BA5065 Air Fryer Oven is another air fryer oven that deserves a top position. It comes with an adjustable thermostat that helps to control the temperature to any level you want. The air fryer has 3 cooking presets that you can set for your favorite foods. The thermostat can also be adjusted by pressing the numbered buttons on the right side of the oven.

Another model on our list of recommended air fryer ovens is the Cuisinart Air Fryer BCO-50. This air fryer oven can be used to make a variety of foods. The cook settings provide slow and fast cooking options for meats, poultry and fish. If your goal is to make delicious food without any stress just like it is done in restaurants, then this air fryer oven is definitely for you. The adjustable thermostat can help you adjust the temperature even more so that you can get a more perfect cooking experience.

The ninja air fryer oven on our list is Ninja Master Cook NE-B16, which is a great choice for people with limited counter space. It measures only 14.9 x 10.6 x 9.3 inches and weighs 9.4 pounds, so this appliance can be placed anywhere in your kitchen but you will still be able to enjoy a high-quality cooking experience. You won't even feel that you have just moved the air fryer oven around because it has great weight distribution making it very convenient to use.

An air fryer oven is still an oven, and therefore you will have to account for the heat of the cooking process. Cooking times may vary. You can use a convection setting on an air fryer oven, and it is often recommended that this be done in order to cook more evenly and quickly. The surface temperature of food cooked in a convection mode is around 240°F, which is also high enough to burn the exterior of food quickly if not taken care of properly. Grilling outside is unhealthy and can create carcinogenic compounds. Using an indoor air fryer is the best way to cook without using oil. Ovens heat food above the temperature required to kill bacteria, while air fryers cook it at temperatures too low to produce those same harmful compounds. Cooking and serving food in air frying ovens reduce cooking time by many times over that of a conventional oven or stovetop.

Using an air fryer to cook is much healthier than using oil and other fats. Using a standard convection oven, it takes about 3 tablespoons of oil to fry a chicken breast. The same chicken cooked in an air fryer takes about 5 tablespoons of oil - that's 25% less! Use just a couple of tsp. of olive oil and you'll be surprised how much flavor you can get out with so little.

Cooking by means of an air fryer can be a healthier alternative to using other oils and fats. The latter are usually tropical in origin and contain saturated fats. To get the same amount of flavor out of last night's steak, you would need 10 times the amount of oil that comes from an air fryer in just a couple of teaspoons!

In grilling using air fryer ovens, you can feed about 10 to 20 people with the air fryer which in comparison to the conventional ovens can only cook 3 to 6 people.

The amount of time required for preparing and cooking a meal in an air fryer is significantly less than that of regular grills, and air fryers do not require much of any oil. Cooking times may differ reliant on the type and quantity of food being cooked, but usually, at temperatures amid 300°F and 400°F, the food will be ready in around 10 minutes.

In baking using air fryer ovens, you can cook at 350°F for around 20 minutes and at 400°F for a little over half that time.

In Roasting using an air fryer oven, you can do a large turkey around 18 pounds. The same in the conventional oven takes 35 to 50 minutes to get the same result, which is best if you want crispy skin.

Breakfast and Brunch

Duo-Cheese Roll

Preparation Time: 10 minutes

Cooking Time: 20 minutes

Servings: 12 rolls

Ingredients:

- 2½ cups shredded Mozzarella cheese
- 2 oz. (57 g) cream cheese, softened
- 1 cup blanched finely ground almond flour
- ½ tsp. vanilla extract
- ½ cup erythritol
- 1 tbsp. ground cinnamon

Directions:

1. In a large microwave-safe bowl, combine Mozzarella cheese, cream cheese, and flour. Microwave the mixture on high for 90 seconds until cheese is melted.
2. Add vanilla extract and erythritol, and mix 2 minutes until a dough form.
3. Once the dough is cool enough to work with your hands, about 2 minutes, spread it out into a 12-inch × 4-inch rectangle on ungreased parchment paper. Evenly sprinkle dough with cinnamon.

4. Starting at the long side of the dough, roll lengthwise to form a log. Slice the log into twelve even pieces.

5. Divide rolls between two ungreased 6-inch round nonstick baking dishes. Place one dish into the air fryer basket. Adjust the temperature to 375°F (190°C) and set the timer for 10 minutes.

6. Cinnamon rolls will be done when golden around the edges and mostly firm. Repeat with the second dish. Allow rolls to cool in dishes 10 minutes before serving.

Nutrition:

Calories: 145 Fat: 10g Protein: 8g Carbs: 10g Net Carbs: 9g Fiber: 1g

Sausage with Peppers

Preparation Time: 15 minutes

Cooking Time: 15 minutes

Servings: 4

Ingredients:

- ½ lb. (227 g) spicy ground pork breakfast sausage
- 4 large eggs
- 4 oz. (113 g) full-fat cream cheese, softened
- ¼ cup canned diced tomatoes and green chiles, drained
- 4 large poblano peppers
- 8 tbsp. shredded pepper jack cheese
- ½ cup full-fat sour cream

Directions:

1. In a medium skillet over medium heat, crumble and brown the ground sausage until no pink remains. Remove sausage and drain the fat from the pan. Crack eggs into the pan, scramble, and cook until no longer runny.

2. Place cooked sausage in a large bowl and fold in cream cheese. Mix in diced tomatoes and chiles. Gently fold in eggs.

3. Cut a 4-inch–5-inch slit in the top of each poblano, removing the seeds and white membrane with a small knife. Separate the filling into four servings and spoon

carefully into each pepper. Top each with 2 tablespoons of pepper jack cheese.

4. Place each pepper into the air fryer basket.
5. Adjust the temperature to 350°F (180°C) and set the timer for 15 minutes.
6. Peppers will be soft and cheese will be browned when ready. Serve immediately with sour cream on top.

Nutrition:

Calories: 489 Fat: 35g Protein: 23g Carbs: 13g Net Carbs: 9g Fiber: 4g

Simple Ham and Pepper Omelet

Preparation Time: 5 minutes

Cooking Time: 8 minutes

Servings: 1

Ingredients:

- 2 large eggs
- ¼ cup unsweetened, unflavored almond milk
- ¼ tsp. fine sea salt
- ⅛ tsp. ground black pepper
- ¼ cup diced ham (omit for vegetarian)
- ¼ cup diced green and red bell peppers
- 2 tbsp. diced green onions, plus more for garnish
- ¼ cup shredded Cheddar cheese (about 1 oz./28g) (omit for dairy-free)
- Quartered cherry tomatoes, for serving (optional)

Directions:

1. Preheat the air fryer to 350°F (180°C). Grease a 6 by 3-inch cake pan and set it aside.
2. In a small bowl, use a fork to whisk together the eggs, almond milk, salt, and pepper. Add the ham, bell peppers, and green onions. Pour the mixture into the greased pan. Add the cheese on top (if using).
3. Place the pan in the basket of the air fryer. Cook for 8 minutes, or until the eggs are cooked to your liking.

4. Loosen the omelet from the sides of the pan with a spatula and place it on a serving plate. Garnish with green onions and Servings with cherry tomatoes, if desired. Best served fresh.

Nutrition:

Calories: 476 Fat: 32g Protein: 41g Carbs: 3g Net Carbs: 2g Fiber: 1g

Air Fryer Baked Eggs

Preparation Time: 5 minutes

Cooking Time: 6 to 7 minutes

Servings: 2

Ingredients:

- 2 large eggs
- 2 tbsp. half-and-half
- 2 tsp. shredded Cheddar cheese
- Salt and freshly ground black pepper, to taste
- Cooking spray

Directions:

1. Spritz 2 ramekins lightly with cooking spray. Crack an egg into each ramekin.
2. Top each egg with 1 tablespoon of half-and-half and 1 teaspoon of Cheddar cheese. Sprinkle with salt and black pepper. Stir the egg mixture with a fork until well combined.
3. Select Bake, set temperature to 330°F (166°C), and set time to 6 minutes. Select Start to begin preheating.
4. Once preheated, place the ramekins in the oven.
5. When cooking is complete, the eggs should be set. Check for doneness and continue cooking for 1 minute more as needed. Allow cooling for 5 minutes before removing and serving.

Nutrition:

Calories: 63 Protein: 3.07 g Fat: 4.71 g Carbohydrates: 1.92 g

Egg in a Hole

Preparation Time: 5 minutes

Cooking Time: 5 minutes

Servings: 1

Ingredients:

- 1 slice bread
- 1 tsp. butter, softened
- 1 egg
- Salt and pepper, to taste
- 1 tbsp. shredded Cheddar cheese
- 2 tsp. diced ham

Directions:

1. On a flat work surface, cut a hole in the center of the bread slice with a 2½-inch-diameter biscuit cutter.
2. Spread the butter evenly on each side of the bread slice and transfer to a baking dish.
3. Crack the egg into the hole and season as desired with salt and pepper. Scatter the shredded cheese and diced ham on top.
4. Select Bake, set temperature to 330°F (166°C), and set time to 5 minutes. Select Start to begin preheating.
5. Once preheated, place the baking dish in the oven.
6. When cooking is complete, the bread should be lightly browned and the egg should be set. Remove from the oven and Servings hot.

Nutrition:

Calories: 235 Protein: 11.45 g Fat: 14.26 g Carbohydrates: 15.36
g

Simple Monkey Bread

Preparation Time: 5 minutes

Cooking Time: 8 minutes

Servings: 4

Ingredients:

- 1 (8-oz./227-g) can refrigerated biscuits
- 3 tbsp. melted unsalted butter
- ¼ cup white sugar
- 3 tbsp. brown sugar
- ½ tsp. cinnamon
- ⅛ tsp. nutmeg

Directions:

1. On a clean work surface, cut each biscuit into 4 pieces.
2. In a shallow bowl, place the melted butter. In another shallow bowl, stir together the white sugar, brown sugar, cinnamon, and nutmeg until combined.
3. Dredge the biscuits, one at a time, in the melted butter, then roll them in the sugar mixture to coat well. Spread the biscuits evenly in a baking pan.
4. Select Bake. Set temperature to 350°F (180°C) and set time to 8 minutes. Select Start to begin preheating.
5. Once the oven has preheated, place the pan into the oven.
6. When cooked, the biscuits should be golden brown.
7. Cool for 5 minutes before serving.

Nutrition:

Calories: 235 Protein: 11.45 g Fat: 14.26 g Carbohydrates: 15.36 g

Breakfast Cheese Sandwiches

Preparation Time: 5 minutes

Cooking Time: 8 minutes

Servings: 2

Ingredients:

- 1 tsp. butter, softened
- 4 slices bread
- 4 slices smoked country ham
- 4 slices Cheddar cheese
- 4 thick slices of tomato

Directions:

1. Spoon ½ teaspoon of butter onto one side of 2 slices of bread and spread it all over.
2. Assemble the sandwiches: Top each of 2 slices of unbuttered bread with 2 slices of ham, 2 slices of cheese, and 2 slices of tomato. Place the remaining 2 slices of bread on top, butter-side up.
3. Lay the sandwiches in a perforated pan, buttered side down.
4. Select Bake, set temperature to 370°F (188°C), and set time to 8 minutes. Select Start to begin preheating.
5. Once preheated, slide the pan into the oven. Flip the sandwiches halfway through the cooking time.
6. When cooking is complete, the sandwiches should be golden brown on both sides and the cheese should be

melted. Remove from the oven. Allow cooling for 5 minutes before slicing to Servings.

Nutrition:

Calories: 405 Protein: 25.18 g Fat: 23.8 g Carbohydrates: 22.58 g

Peppered Maple Bacon Knots

Preparation Time: 5 minutes

Cooking Time: 7 to 8 minutes

Servings: 6

Ingredients:

- 1 lb. (454 g) maple smoked center-cut bacon
- ¼ cup maple syrup
- ¼ cup brown sugar
- Coarsely cracked black peppercorns, to taste

Directions:

1. On a clean work surface, tie each bacon strip in a loose knot.
2. Stir together the maple syrup and brown sugar in a bowl. Generously brush this mixture over the bacon knots.
3. Place the bacon knots in a perforated pan and sprinkle with the coarsely cracked black peppercorns.
4. Select Air Fry, set temperature to 390°F (199°C), and set time to 8 minutes. Select Start to begin preheating.
5. Once preheated, slide the pan into the oven.
6. After 5 minutes, remove the pan from the oven and flip the bacon knots. Return the pan to the oven and continue cooking for 2 to 3 minutes more.
7. When cooking is complete, the bacon should be crisp. Remove from the oven to a paper towel-lined plate. Let the bacon knots cool for a few minutes and Serve warm.

Nutrition:

Calories: 303 Protein: 8.09 g Fat: 22.33 g Carbohydrates: 22.57 g

Snack and Appetizers

Flavors Chicken Tandoori

Preparation Time: 10 minutes

Cooking Time: 15 minutes

Servings: 4

Ingredients:

- 1 lb. chicken tenders, cut in half
- ¼ cup parsley, chopped
- 1 tbsp. garlic, minced
- 1 tbsp. ginger, minced
- 1 tsp. paprika
- 1 tsp. garam masala
- 1 tsp. turmeric
- 1 tsp. cayenne pepper
- ¼ cup yogurt
- 1 tsp. salt

Directions:

1. Preheat the Air Fryer Oven to 350°F.
2. Add all ingredients into the large bowl and mix well. Place in refrigerator for 30 minutes.
3. Spray air fryer basket with cooking spray.
4. Add marinated chicken into the air fryer basket and cook for 15 minutes. Turn chicken after 10 minutes.

5. Servings and enjoy.

Nutrition:

Calories 240 Fat 8.9 g Carbohydrates 3.9 g Sugar 1.3 g Protein 34.2 g Cholesterol 102 mg

Chicken Kabab

Preparation Time: 10 minutes

Cooking Time: 6 minutes

Servings: 3

Ingredients:

- 1 lb. ground chicken
- 2 green onions, chopped
- 1 egg, lightly beaten
- 1/3 cup fresh parsley, chopped
- 2 garlic cloves
- 4 oz. onion, chopped
- ¼ tsp. turmeric powder
- ½ tsp. black pepper
- 1 tbsp. fresh lemon juice
- ¼ cup almond flour

Directions:

1. Spray air fryer basket with cooking spray.
2. Add all ingredients into the food processor and process until well combined.
3. Transfer chicken mixture to the mixing bowl and place it in the refrigerator for 30 minutes.
4. Divide mixture into the 6 equal portions and roll around the skewers.
5. Place kabab into the air fryer basket and cook at 400°F for 6 minutes.

6. Servings and enjoy.

Nutrition:

Calories 348 Fat 14 g Carbohydrates 6.4 g Sugar 2.2 g Protein 47.1 g Cholesterol 189 mg

Steamed Pot Stickers

Preparation Time: 20minutes

Cooking Time: 10 minutes

Servings: 30 Pot Stickers

Ingredients:

- ½ cup finely chopped cabbage
- ¼ cup finely chopped red bell pepper
- 2 green onions, finely chopped
- 1 egg, beaten
- 2 tbsp. cocktail sauce
- 2 tsp. low-sodium soy sauce
- 30 wonton wrappers
- 3 tbsp. water, plus more for brushing the wrappers

Directions:

1. In a small bowl, combine the cabbage, pepper, green onions, egg, cocktail sauce, and soy sauce, and mix well.

2. Put about 1 teaspoon of the mixture in the center of each wonton wrapper. Fold the wrapper in half, covering the filling; dampen the edges with water, and seal. You can crimp the edges of the wrapper with your fingers so they look like the pot-stickers you get in restaurants. Brush them with water.

3. Put 3 tablespoons of water in the pan under the air fryer basket. Cook the pot-stickers in 2 batches for 9 to 10

minutes or until the pot-stickers are hot and the bottoms are lightly browned.

Substitution tip: Use other vegetables in this recipe, such as corn, baby peas, or chopped zucchini or summer squash. You could also add leftover cooked meat such as pork or chicken, finely chopped.

Nutrition: (3 post-stickers):

Calories: 291; Total Fat: 2 g Saturated Fat: 0 g Cholesterol: 35 mg Sodium: 649 mg Carbohydrates: 57 g Fiber: 3 g Protein: 10g

Beef and Mango Skewers

Preparation Time: 10 minutes

Cooking Time: 4 to 7 minutes

Servings: 4

Ingredients:

- ¾ lb. beef sirloin tip, cut into 1-inch cubes
- 2 tbsp. balsamic vinegar
- 1 tbsp. olive oil
- 1 tbsp. honey
- ½ tsp. dried marjoram
- Pinch salt
- Freshly ground black pepper
- 1 mango

Directions:

1. Put the beef cubes in a medium bowl and add the balsamic vinegar, olive oil, honey, marjoram, salt, and pepper. Mix well, then massage the marinade into the beef with your hands. Set aside.

2. To prepare the mango, stand it on end and cut the skin off, using a sharp knife. Then carefully cut around the oval pit to remove the flesh. Cut the mango into 1-inch cubes.

3. Thread metal skewers alternating with three beef cubes and two mango cubes.

4. Grill the skewers in the air fryer basket for 4 to 7 minutes or until the beef is browned and at least 145°F.

Nutrition:

Calories: 242; Total Fat: 9 g Saturated Fat: 3 g Cholesterol: 76 mg Sodium: 96 mg Carbohydrates: 13 g Fiber: 1 g Protein: 26g

Curried Sweet Potato Fries

Preparation Time: 5 minutes

Cooking Time: 8-12 minutes

Servings: 4

Ingredients:

- ½ cup sour cream
- ½ cup mango chutney
- 3 tsp. curry powder, divided
- 4 cups frozen sweet potato fries
- 1 tbsp. olive oil
- Pinch salt
- Freshly ground black pepper

Directions:

1. In a small bowl, combine sour cream, chutney, and 1½ teaspoons of the curry powder. Mix well and set aside.

2. Put the sweet potatoes in a medium bowl. Drizzle with the olive oil and sprinkle with the remaining 1½ teaspoons curry powder, salt, and pepper.

3. Put the potatoes in the air fryer basket. Cook for 8 to 12 minutes or until crisp, hot, and golden brown, shaking the basket once during cooking time.

4. Place the fries in a serving basket and Servings with the chutney dip.

Substitution tip: You can use fresh sweet potatoes in place of the frozen precut fries. Use one or two sweet potatoes, peel them and cut into 1/3-inch-thick strips using a sharp knife or mandoline. Use as directed in the recipe, but you will need to increase the cooking time.

Nutrition:

Calories: 323; Total Fat: 10 g Saturated Fat: 4 g Cholesterol: 13 mg Sodium: 138 mg Carbohydrates: 58 g Fiber: 7 g Protein: 3g

Spicy Kale Chips with Yogurt Sauce

Preparation Time: 10 minutes

Cooking Time: 5 minutes

Servings: 4

Ingredients:

- 1 cup Greek yogurt
- 3 tbsp. lemon juice
- 2 tbsp. honey mustard
- ½ tsp. dried oregano
- 1 bunch curly kale
- 2 tbsp. olive oil
- ½ tsp. salt
- ⅛ tsp. pepper

Directions:

1. In a small bowl, combine the yogurt, lemon juice, honey mustard, and oregano, and set aside.
2. Remove the stems and ribs from the kale with a sharp knife. Cut the leaves into 2- to 3-inch pieces.
3. Toss the kale with olive oil, salt, and pepper. Massage the oil into the leaves with your hands.
4. Air-fry the kale in batches until crisp, about 5 minutes, shaking the basket once during cooking time. Servings with the yogurt sauce.

Nutrition:

Calories: 154; Total Fat: 8 g Saturated Fat: 2 g Cholesterol: 3 mg
Sodium: 378 mg Carbohydrates: 13 g Fiber: 1 g Protein: 8g

Phyllo Artichoke Triangles

Preparation Time: 15 minutes

Cooking Time: 9 minutes

Servings: 18 triangles

Ingredients:

- ¼ cup ricotta cheese
- 1 egg white
- 1/3 cup minced drained artichoke hearts
- 3 tbsp. grated mozzarella cheese
- ½ tsp. dried thyme
- 6 sheets frozen phyllo dough, thawed
- 2 tbsp. melted butter

Directions:

1. In a small bowl, combine ricotta cheese, egg white, artichoke hearts, mozzarella cheese, and thyme, and mix well.

2. Cover the phyllo dough with a damp kitchen towel while you work so it doesn't dry out. Using one sheet at a time, place on the work surface and cut into thirds lengthwise.

3. Put about 1½ teaspoons of the filling on each strip at the base. Fold the bottom right-hand tip of phyllo over the filling to meet the other side in a triangle, then continue folding in a triangle. Brush each triangle with butter to seal the edges. Repeat with remaining phyllo dough and filling.

4. Bake, 6 at a time, for about 3 to 4 minutes or until the phyllo is golden brown and crisp.

Substitution tip: You can use anything in this filling in place of the artichoke hearts. Try spinach, chopped cooked shrimp, cooked sausage, or keep it vegetarian and use all grated cheese.

Nutrition: (3 triangles):

Calories: 271; Total Fat: 17 g Saturated Fat: 7 g Cholesterol: 19 mg Sodium: 232 mg Carbohydrates: 23 g Fiber: 5 g Protein: 9g

Fish and Seafood

Mediterranean Flounder

Preparation Time: 20 minutes

Cooking Time: 12 minutes

Servings: 5

Ingredients:

- 1¾ lbs. salmon fillets
- ¼ tsp. salt
- 1 tsp. smoked paprika
- 1 tsp. ground dried ginger
- ¼ cup pitted olives
- ¼ cup sundried tomatoes
- ¼ cup capers
- 1 tbsp. fresh chopped dill
- 1/3 cup keto pesto sauce

Directions:

1. Preheat your air fryer to 400°F and line your air fryer tray with a long piece of parchment paper.
2. Place the flounder fillets on the parchment and sprinkle with the salt, paprika, and ginger and rub the spices into the fish.

3. Top the fish with the remaining ingredients and then wrap the parchment paper up around the fish fillets, enclosing them completely.

4. Place the tray in the air fryer and bake for 12 minutes.

5. Remove from the air fryer, unwrap the parchment and Servings while hot!

Nutrition:

Calories 211, Total Fat 8 g Saturated Fat 3 g Total Carbs 6 g Net Carbs 3 g Protein 33 g Sugar 1 g Fiber 3 g Sodium 489 mg Potassium 321 g

Tomato Parchment Cod

Preparation Time: 20 minutes

Cooking Time: 15 minutes

Servings: 5

Ingredients:

- 1¾ lbs. cod fillets
- ¼ tsp. salt
- 1 tsp. smoked paprika
- 1 tsp. ground dried ginger
- ¼ cup pitted olives
- ¼ cup sundried tomatoes
- ¼ cup capers
- 1 tbsp. fresh chopped dill
- 1/3 cup keto marinara

Directions:

1. Preheat your air fryer to 400°F and line your air fryer tray with a long piece of parchment paper.
2. Place the cod fillets on the parchment and sprinkle with the salt, paprika, and ginger and rub the spices into the fish.
3. Top the fish with the remaining ingredients and then wrap the parchment paper up around the fish fillets, enclosing them completely.
4. Place the tray in the air fryer and bake for 15 minutes.

5. Remove from the air fryer, unwrap the parchment, and Servings while hot!

Nutrition:

Calories 373, Total Fat 7 g Saturated Fat 3 g Total Carbs 5 g Net Carbs 3 g Protein 33 g Sugar 1 g Fiber 2 g Sodium 489 mg Potassium 321 g

Italian Style Flounder

Preparation Time: 20 minutes

Cooking Time: 15 minutes

Servings: 5

Ingredients:

- 1¾ lbs. salmon fillets
- ¼ tsp. salt
- 2 tsp. Italian seasoning
- 1 cup baby spinach
- ¼ cup sundried tomatoes
- 1 tbsp. fresh chopped dill
- 1/3 cup keto pesto sauce

Directions:

1. Preheat your air fryer to 400°F and line your air fryer tray with a long piece of parchment paper.
2. Place the flounder fillets on the parchment and sprinkle with the salt and Italian seasoning and rub the spices into the fish.
3. Top the fish with the remaining ingredients and then wrap the parchment paper up around the fish fillets, enclosing them completely.
4. Place the tray in the air fryer and bake for 20 minutes.
5. Remove from the air fryer, unwrap the parchment, and Servings while hot!

Nutrition:

Calories 226, Total Fat 8 g Saturated Fat 3 g Total Carbs 7 g Net Carbs 3 g Protein 30 g Sugar 2 g Fiber 4 g Sodium 487 mg Potassium 321 g

Prosciutto Wrapped Ahi

Preparation Time: 5 minutes

Cooking Time: 20 minutes

Servings: 2

Ingredients:

- 1 lb. cod Ahi
- ¼ tsp. salt
- ¼ tsp. ground black pepper
- 2 oz. prosciutto di parma, very thinly sliced
- 2 tbsp. olive oil
- 1 tsp. minced garlic
- 4 cups baby spinach
- 2 tsp. lemon juice

Directions:

1. Preheat your air fryer to 325°F and line your air fryer tray with foil.
2. Dry the cod fillets by patting with a paper towel, sprinkle with salt and pepper.
3. Wrap the fillets in the prosciutto, enclosing them as fully as possible.
4. Place the wrapped fillets on the prepared tray.
5. Place the tray in the air fryer and bake for 10 minutes.
6. Toss the spinach with olive oil, garlic and lemon juice and remove the tray from the air fryer and place the spinach mix on the tray as well, around the wrapped cod.

7. Place in the air fryer and bake for another 10 minutes. The spinach should be nicely wilted and the fish 145°F internally.

8. Servings hot!

Nutrition:

Calories 420, Total Fat 20 g Saturated Fat 4 g Total Carbs 11 g Net Carbs 9 g Protein 49 g Sugar 3 g Fiber 2 g Sodium 480 mg Potassium 579 g

Vegetable

Simple Ricotta & Spinach Balls

Preparation Time: 5 minutes

Cooking Time: 12 minutes

Servings: 4

Ingredients:

- 14 oz. store-bought crescent dough
- 1 cup steamed spinach
- 1 cup crumbled ricotta cheese
- ¼ tsp. garlic powder
- 1 tsp. chopped oregano
- ¼ tsp. salt

Directions:

1. Preheat on Air Fry function to 350°F. Rolls the dough onto a lightly floured flat surface. Combine the ricotta cheese, spinach, oregano, salt, and garlic powder in a bowl. Cut the dough into four equal pieces.

2. Divide the spinach/feta mixture between the dough pieces. Make sure to place the filling in the center. Fold the dough and secure it with a fork. Place onto a lined baking dish and then in your oven. Cook for 12 minutes until lightly browned. Serve.

Nutrition:

Calories: 135 Protein: 8.45 g Fat: 8.27 g Carbohydrates: 7.8 g

Baby Spinach & Pumpkin with Nuts & Cheese

Preparation Time: 10 minutes

Cooking Time: 25 minutes

Servings: 1

Ingredients:

- ½ small pumpkin
- 2 oz. blue cheese, crumbled
- 2 tbsp. pine nuts
- 1 tbsp. olive oil
- ½ cup baby spinach, packed
- 1 spring onion, sliced
- 1 radish, thinly sliced
- 1 tsp. vinegar

Directions:

1. Preheat on Toast function to 330°F. Place the pine nuts in the Air Fryer pan and toast them for 5 minutes; set aside. Peel the pumpkin and then chop it into small pieces and toss them with olive oil. Place in the Air Fryer basket and fit in the baking tray. Increase the temperature to 390°F and cook for 20 minutes.

2. Remove the pumpkin to a serving bowl. Add in baby spinach, radish, and spring onion; toss with the vinegar. Stir in the blue cheese and top with the toasted pine nuts to serve.

Nutrition:

Calories: 413 Protein: 17.48 g Fat: 30.9 g Carbohydrates: 20.01 g

Sandwiches with Tomato, Nuts & Cheese

Preparation Time: 10 minutes

Cooking Time: 42 minutes

Servings: 2

Ingredients:

- 1 heirloom tomato
- 1 (4-oz.) block feta cheese
- 1 small red onion, thinly sliced
- 1 clove garlic
- Salt to taste
- 2 tsp. + ¼ cup olive oil
- 1½ tbsp. toasted pine nuts
- ¼ cup chopped parsley
- ¼ cup grated Parmesan cheese
- ¼ cup chopped basil

Directions:

1. Add basil, pine nuts, garlic, and salt to a food processor. Process while slowly adding ¼ cup of olive oil. Once finished, pour basil pesto into a bowl and refrigerate for 30 minutes.

2. Preheat on Air Fry function to 390°F. Slice the feta cheese and tomato into ½-inch slices. Remove the pesto from the fridge and spread half of it on the tomato slices. Top with feta cheese slices and onion. Drizzle the remaining olive oil on top.

3. Place the tomatoes in the fryer basket and fit in the baking tray; cook for 12 minutes. Remove to a serving platter and top with the remaining pesto. Serve.

Nutrition:

Calories: 1977 Protein: 4.63 g Fat: 219.77 g Carbohydrates: 4.57 g

Poultry

Restaurant-Style Fried Chicken

Preparation Time: 10 minutes

Cooking Time: 12 minutes

Servings: 4

Ingredients:

- 1 lb. chicken fillets
- 1 egg
- 1 tbsp. olive oil
- 1 cup crackers, crushed
- 1 tbsp. fresh coriander, minced
- 1 tbsp. fresh parsley, minced
- Sea salt and ground black pepper, to taste
- ¼ tsp. ground cumin
- ¼ tsp. mustard seeds
- 1 tsp. celery seeds

Directions:

1. Pat the chicken fillets dry with paper towels. Whisk the egg in a shallow bowl.
2. Mix the remaining ingredients in a separate shallow bowl.
3. Dip the chicken breasts into the egg mixture. Then, roll the chicken breasts over the breadcrumb mixture.

4. Cook the chicken at 380°F for 12 minutes, turning them over halfway through the cooking time.

5. Bon appétit!

Nutrition:

318 Calories; 23.3g Fat; 2.1g Carbs; 23.7g Protein; 0.8g Sugars; 0.3g Fiber

Old-Fashioned Chicken Schnitzel

Preparation Time: 5 minutes

Cooking Time: 20 minutes

Servings: 3

Ingredients:

- 3 chicken legs, boneless and skinless
- 2 tbsp. olive oil
- 1 tsp. dried basil
- 1 tsp. dried oregano
- 1 tsp. dried sage
- Sea salt and freshly cracked black pepper
- ½ cup breadcrumbs

Directions:

1. Pat the chicken dry with paper towels. Toss the chicken legs with the remaining ingredients.
2. Cook the chicken at 370°F for 20 minutes, turning them over halfway through the cooking time.
3. Bon appétit!

Nutrition:

477 Calories; 21.2g Fat; 14.8g Carbs; 53.3g Protein; 1.9g Sugars; 1.4g Fiber

Mozzarella Stuffed Chicken

Preparation Time: 5 minutes

Cooking Time: 20 minutes

Servings: 4

Ingredients:

- 1 lb. chicken breasts, boneless, skinless, cut into four pieces
- 2 tbsp. sundried tomatoes, chopped
- 1 garlic clove, minced
- 2 oz. mozzarella cheese, crumbled
- Sea salt and ground black pepper, to taste
- 1 tbsp. olive oil

Directions:

1. Flatten the chicken breasts with a mallet.
2. Stuff each piece of chicken with sundried tomatoes, garlic, and cheese. Roll them up and secure with toothpicks.
3. Season the chicken with salt and pepper and drizzle the olive oil over them.
4. Place the stuffed chicken in the Air Fryer cooking basket. Cook the chicken at 400°F for about 20 minutes, turning them over halfway through the cooking time.
5. Bon appétit

Nutrition:

257 Calories; 13.9g Fat; 2.7g Carbs; 28.3g Protein; 1.4g Sugars; 0.6g Fiber

Balsamic Chicken Drumettes

Preparation Time: 10 minutes

Cooking Time: 22 minutes

Servings: 4

Ingredients:

- 1½ lbs. chicken drumettes
- 2 tbsp. olive oil
- 2 tbsp. balsamic vinegar
- Kosher salt and ground black pepper, to taste

Directions:

1. Toss the chicken drumettes with the remaining ingredients.
2. Cook the chicken drumettes at 380°F for 22 minutes, turning them over halfway through the cooking time.
3. Bon appétit!

Nutrition:

265 Calories; 11.4g Fat; 2.4g Carbs; 34.4g Protein; 1.7g Sugars; 0.2g Fiber

Meat

Beef Cheeseburger Egg Rolls

Preparation Time: 15 minutes

Cooking Time: 8 minutes

Servings: 6 egg rolls

Ingredients:

- 8 oz. (227 g) raw lean ground beef
- ½ cup chopped onion
- ½ cup chopped bell pepper
- ¼ tsp. onion powder
- ¼ tsp. garlic powder
- 3 tbsp. cream cheese
- 1 tbsp. yellow mustard
- 3 tbsp. shredded Cheddar cheese
- 6 chopped dill pickle chips
- 6-egg roll wrappers

Directions:

1. Preheat the air fryer to 392°F (200°C).
2. In a skillet, add the beef, onion, bell pepper, onion powder, and garlic powder. Stir and crumble beef until fully cooked, and vegetables are soft.
3. Take the skillet off the heat and add cream cheese, mustard, and Cheddar cheese, stirring until melted.

4. Pour beef mixture into a bowl and fold in pickles.

5. Lay out egg wrappers and divide the beef mixture into each one. Moisten egg roll wrapper edges with water. Fold sides to the middle and seal with water.

6. Repeat with all other egg rolls.

7. Put rolls into an air fryer, one batch at a time. Air fry for 8 minutes.

8. Serve immediately.

Nutrition:

Calories: 211 Protein: 14.08 g Fat: 6.96 g Carbohydrates: 21.95 g

Chicken Fried Steak

Preparation Time: 15 minutes

Cooking Time: 10 minutes

Servings: 4

Ingredients:

- ½ cup flour
- 2 tsp. salt, divided
- Freshly ground black pepper, to taste
- ¼ tsp. garlic powder
- 1 cup buttermilk
- 1 cup fine bread crumbs
- 4 (6-oz./170-g) tenderized top round steaks, ½-inch thick
- Vegetable or canola oil

For the Gravy:

1. 2 tbsp. butter or bacon drippings
2. ¼ onion, minced
3. 1 clove garlic, smashed
4. ¼ tsp. dried thyme
5. 3 tbsp. flour
6. 1 cup milk
7. Salt and freshly ground black pepper, to taste
8. Dashes of Worcestershire sauce

Directions:

1. Set up a dredging station. Combine the flour, 1 teaspoon of salt, black pepper and garlic powder in a shallow bowl. Pour the buttermilk into a second shallow bowl. Finally, put the bread crumbs and 1 teaspoon of salt in a third shallow bowl.

2. Dip the tenderized steaks into the flour, then the buttermilk, and then the bread crumb mixture, pressing the crumbs onto the steak. Put them on a baking sheet and spray both sides generously with vegetable or canola oil.

3. Preheat the air fryer to 400°F (204°C).

4. Transfer the steaks to the air fryer basket, two at a time, and air fry for 10 minutes, flipping the steaks over halfway through the cooking time. Hold the first batch of steaks warm in a 170°F (77°C) oven while you air fry the second batch.

5. While the steaks are cooking, make the gravy. Melt the butter in a small saucepan over medium heat on the stovetop. Add the onion, garlic and thyme and cook for five minutes, until the onion is soft and just starting to brown. Stir in the flour and cook for another five minutes, stirring regularly, until the mixture starts to brown. Whisk in the milk and bring the mixture to a boil to thicken. Season to taste with salt, lots of freshly

ground black pepper, and a few dashes of Worcestershire sauce.

6. Pour the gravy over the chicken fried steaks and serve.

Nutrition:

Calories: 654 Protein: 87.05 g Fat: 19.16 g Carbohydrates: 27.61 g

Super Bacon with Meat

Preparation Time: 5 minutes

Preparation Time: 1 hour 25 minutes

Cooking Time: 1 hour

Servings: 4

Ingredients:

- 30 slices thick-cut bacon
- 4 oz. (113 g) Cheddar cheese, shredded
- 12 oz. (340 g) steak
- 10 oz. (283 g) pork sausage
- Salt and ground black pepper, to taste

Directions:

1. Preheat the air fryer to 400°F (204°C).
2. Lay out 30 slices of bacon in a woven pattern and bake for 20 minutes until crisp. Put the cheese in the center of the bacon.
3. Combine the steak and sausage to form a meaty mixture.
4. Lay out the meat in a rectangle of similar size to the bacon strips. Season with salt and pepper.
5. Roll the meat into a tight roll and refrigerate.
6. Preheat the air fryer to 400°F (204°C).
7. Make a 7×7 bacon weave and roll the bacon weave over the meat, diagonally.
8. Bake for 60 minutes or until the internal temperature reaches at least 165°F (74°C).

9. Let rest for 5 minutes before serving.

Nutrition:

Calories: 1178 Protein: 59.35 g Fat: 101.47 g Carbohydrates: 6.5 g

Sun-Dried Tomato Crusted Chops

Preparation Time: 15 minutes

Cooking Time: 10 minutes

Servings: 4

Ingredients:

- ½ cup oil-packed sun-dried tomatoes
- ½ cup toasted almonds
- ¼ cup grated Parmesan cheese
- ½ cup olive oil, plus more for brushing the air fryer basket
- 2 tbsp. water
- ½ tsp. salt
- Freshly ground black pepper, to taste
- 4 center-cut boneless pork chops (about 1¼ lbs./567 g)

Directions:

1. Put the sun-dried tomatoes into a food processor and pulse them until they are coarsely chopped. Add the almonds, Parmesan cheese, olive oil, water, salt and pepper. Process into a smooth paste. Spread most of the paste (leave a little in reserve) onto both sides of the pork chops and then pierce the meat several times with a needle-style meat tenderizer or a fork. Let the pork chops sit and marinate for at least 1 hour (refrigerate if marinating for longer than 1 hour).

2. Preheat the air fryer to 370°F (188°C).

---

3. Brush more olive oil on the bottom of the air fryer basket. Transfer the pork chops into the air fryer basket, spooning a little more of the sun-dried tomato paste onto the pork chops if there are any gaps where the paste may have been rubbed off. Air fry the pork chops for 10 minutes, turning the chops over halfway through.
4. When the pork chops have finished cooking, transfer them to a serving plate and serve.

Nutrition:

Calories: 295 Protein: 2.5 g Fat: 30.75 g Carbohydrates: 4.11 g

Vegan and Vegetarian

Authentic Vegan Ratatouille

Preparation Time: 10 minutes

Cooking Time: 15 minutes

Servings: 2

Ingredients:

- 4 oz. courgette, sliced
- 4 oz. eggplant, sliced
- 1 bell pepper, sliced
- 4 oz. tomatoes, peeled and quartered
- 1 yellow onion, peeled and sliced
- 1 tsp. fresh garlic, minced
- ½ tsp. oregano
- ½ tsp. basil
- Coarse sea salt and ground black pepper, to taste
- 1 tbsp. olive oil

Directions:

1. Place the sliced veggies in the Air Fryer cooking basket. Season your veggies with oregano, basil, salt and black pepper. Drizzle olive oil over the top.
2. Cook your veggies at 400°F for about 15 minutes, shaking the basket halfway through the cooking time to promote even cooking.

3. Arrange the sliced veggies in alternating patterns and serve warm. Bon appétit!

Nutrition:

136 Calories; 7.4g Fat; 16g Carbs; 3.7g Protein; 8.3g Sugars

Peppers Provençal with Garbanzo Beans

Preparation Time: 10 minutes

Cooking Time: 25 minutes

Servings: 3

Ingredients:

- 1 lb. bell peppers, deseeded and sliced
- 2 tsp. olive oil
- 1 tsp. Herbs de Provence
- 1 onion, chopped
- 10 oz. canned tomato sauce
- 1 tsp. red wine vinegar
- 9 oz. canned garbanzo beans

Directions:

1. Drizzle the bell peppers with 1 teaspoon of olive oil; sprinkle them with Herbs de Provence and transfer to the Air Fryer cooking basket.

2. Cook the peppers in the preheated Air Fryer at 400°F for 15 minutes, shaking the basket halfway through the cooking time.

3. Meanwhile, heat the remaining teaspoon of olive oil in a saucepan over medium-high heat. Once hot, sauté the onion until just tender and translucent.

4. Then, add in the tomato sauce and let it simmer, partially covered, for about 10 minutes until the sauce has

thickened. Remove from the heat and add in the vinegar and garbanzo beans; stir to combine.

5. Serve the roasted peppers with the saucy garbanzo beans. Bon appétit!

Nutrition:

236 Calories; 5.9g Fat; 40.1g Carbs; 10.1g Protein; 15.1g Sugars

Crispy Garlic Tofu with Brussels Sprouts

Preparation Time: 10 minutes

Cooking Time: 20 minutes

Servings: 2

Ingredients:

- 8 oz. firm tofu, pressed and cut into bite-sized cubes
- 1 tsp. garlic paste
- 1 tbsp. arrowroot powder
- 1 tsp. peanut oil
- ½ lb. Brussels sprouts, halved
- Sea salt and ground black pepper, to taste

Directions:

1. Toss the tofu cubes with garlic paste, arrowroot powder and peanut oil.
2. Transfer your tofu to the Air Fryer cooking basket; add in the Brussels sprouts and season everything with salt and black pepper.
3. Cook the tofu cubes and Brussels sprouts at 380°F for 15 minutes, shaking the basket halfway through the cooking time. Bon appétit!

Nutrition:

256 Calories; 12.5g Fat; 21.1g Carbs; 22.8g Protein; 3.6g Sugars

Baby Potatoes with Garlic-Rosemary Sauce

Preparation Time: 10 minutes

Cooking Time: 50 minutes

Servings: 3

Ingredients:

- 1 lb. baby potatoes, scrubbed
- 1 tbsp. olive oil
- ½ garlic bulb, slice the top ¼-inch off the garlic head
- 1 tbsp. fresh rosemary leaves, chopped
- 1 tsp. sherry vinegar
- ½ cup white wine
- Salt and freshly ground black pepper

Directions:

1. Brush the baby potatoes with olive oil and transfer them to the air Fryer cooking basket. Cook the baby potatoes at 400°F for 12 minutes, shaking the basket halfway through the cooking time.

2. Place the garlic bulb into the center of a piece of aluminum foil. Drizzle the garlic bulb with a nonstick cooking spray and wrap tightly in foil.

3. Cook the garlic at 390°F for about 25 minutes or until the cloves are tender.

4. Let it cool for about 10 minutes; remove the cloves by squeezing them out of the skins; mash the garlic and add it to a saucepan.

5. Stir the remaining ingredients into the saucepan and let it simmer for 10 to 15 minutes until the sauce has reduced by half. Spoon the sauce over the baby potatoes and serve warm. Bon appétit!

Nutrition:

166 Calories; 4.6g Fat; 28.1g Carbs; 3.5g Protein; 1.6g Sugars

Golden Beet Salad with Tahini Sauce

Preparation Time: 10 minutes

Cooking Time: 40 minutes

Servings: 2

Ingredients:

- 2 golden beets
- 1 tbsp. sesame oil
- Sea salt and ground black pepper, to taste
- 2 cups baby spinach
- 2 tbsp. tahini
- 2 tbsp. soy sauce
- 1 tbsp. white vinegar
- 1 clove garlic, pressed
- ½ jalapeno pepper, chopped
- ¼ tsp. ground cumin

Directions:

1. Toss the golden beets with sesame oil. Cook the golden beets in the preheated Air Fryer at 400°F for 40 minutes, turning them over once or twice to ensure even cooking.

2. Let your beets cool completely and then, slice them with a sharp knife. Place the beets in a salad bowl and add in salt, pepper and baby spinach.

3. In a small mixing dish, whisk the remaining ingredients until well combined.

4. Spoon the sauce over your beets, toss to combine, and serve immediately. Bon appétit!

Nutrition:

253 Calories; 18.1g Fat; 19.1g Carbs; 6.4g Protein; 10.1g Sugars

Dessert

Donuts

Preparation Time: 10 minutes

Cooking Time: 120 minutes

Servings: 14 donuts

Ingredients:

- 3 cups of all-purpose flour
- 1 cup of milk, warmed to around 110°F
- 4 tbsp. of unsalted melted butter
- 1 large egg
- ¼ cup +1 tsp. of sugar
- 2½ tsp. of active dry yeast
- ½ tsp. of kosher salt

For Glaze:

- 2 cups of powdered sugar
- 6 tbsp. of unsalted melted butter
- 2 tsp. of vanilla extract
- 2–4 tbsp. of hot water

Directions:

1. Add the warm milk, yeast, and 1 teaspoon of sugar to a large bowl. Stir it for 5–10 minutes until foamy.

2. Add the egg, ¼ cup of sugar, and salt into the milk mixture. Stir it until combined. Pour in the melted butter with 2 cups of flour and mix.

3. Scrape the sides of the bowl down, and add in 1 more cup of flour. Mix it well until the dough starts pulling away from the bowl but leaves sticky. Continue kneading for 5–10 minutes. Cover the bowl with plastic wrap. Leave it for 30 minutes until the dough doubled.

4. Spread some flour on the work surface. Transfer the dough onto it and roll into a ½-¼-inch-thick layer. Cut out donuts with a round cutter (about 3 inches in diameter). Use a smaller cutter (about 1 inch in diameter) and cut out the centers.

5. Transfer the formed donuts onto the oiled parchment paper, and cover them with oiled plastic wrap. Leave it for 20–30 minutes until the dough is doubled.

6. Preheat your air fryer to 350°F. Spray the inside of the basket with some oil.

7. Put the formed donuts in the preheated air fryer in a single layer. Avoid them touching. Lightly spray tops with oil. Cook at 350°F for 4–5 minutes. Repeat this step with the remaining part of donuts and their holes.

8. For making glaze: Meantime, pour the melted butter into a medium bowl. Add in vanilla and powdered sugar. Whisk until combined. Stir in 1 tablespoon of hot water at a time until you reach the desired consistency.

———

9. After cooling the cooked donuts for a few minutes, glaze them until fully coated. Put donuts on the rack to drip off the excess of the glaze until it hardens.

10. Serve and enjoy your Donuts!

Nutrition:

Calories: 270 Carbohydrates: 32 g Fat: 14 g Protein: 3 g Sugar: 17 g Sodium: 70 mg Cholesterol: 25mg

S'mores

Preparation Time: 10 minutes

Cooking Time: 15 minutes

Servings: 4 s'mores

Ingredients:

- 4 marshmallows
- 4 graham crackers, divided in half
- 1 milk chocolate, divided

Directions:

1. Put 4 halves of graham crackers into the air fryer basket.
2. Cut off a small piece from the bottom of each marshmallow and put the marshmallow on the crackers, which will help to stick them well.
3. Cook at 375°F for 7–8 minutes until golden-brown.
4. Add on the top the pieces of chocolate and cover with another half of crackers.
5. Continue cooking for about 2 minutes until the chocolate starts melting.
6. Serve and enjoy your S'mores!

Nutrition: (1 S'more):

Calories: 152 Carbohydrates: 25 g Fat: 5.5 g Protein: 2.2 g Sugar: 16.2 g Sodium: 102 mg Cholesterol: 4 mg

Chocolate Lava Cake

Preparation Time: 10 minutes

Cooking Time: 25 minutes

Servings: 6

Ingredients:

- 8 oz. of baking chocolate bar (about 60% cacao)
- 3 egg yolks
- 3 large eggs
- 1½ cups of powdered sugar
- ½ cup of all-purpose flour
- 10 tbsp. of unsalted butter
- ½ tsp. of salt

Directions:

1. Preheat your air fryer to 400°F.
2. Grease with some oil 6 oven-safe 6-ounce ramekins.
3. Divide the chocolate into small pieces and put them into a medium bowl. Add in butter. Put in a microwave on medium heat power for 90 seconds, stirring every 30 seconds, until you reach a smooth consistency.
4. Add in flour, sugar, and salt. Mix it until well combined.
5. Whisk in eggs and egg yolks. Your batter should become thick but still pourable.
6. Pour all the prepared batter into the ramekins. Put as many ramekins as it can stand in your air fryer basket.

7. Cook at 400°F for 8 minutes (for a runny center) or 10 minutes (for a thicker one). Remove from the basket and leave it for at least 2 minutes.

8. Serve warm and enjoy your Chocolate Lava Cake!

Nutrition: (1 Serving):

Calories: 510 Carbohydrates: 62 g Fat: 29 g Protein: 7 g Sugar: 48 g Sodium: 290 mg Cholesterol: 200mg

Chocolate Chip Cookies

Preparation Time: 10 minutes

Cooking Time: 40 minutes

Servings: 10 cookies

Ingredients:

- 1 cup of all-purpose flour
- ¼ cup of rolled oats
- 1 cup of semi-sweet chocolate chips
- ½ cup of chopped walnuts
- 1/3 cup of brown sugar
- 1/3 cup of granulated sugar
- 8 tbsp. of softened butter
- 1 large egg
- 1 tsp. of vanilla extract
- ½ tsp. of salt
- ½ tsp. of baking soda
- ¼ tsp. of cinnamon
- ⅛ tsp. of lemon juice

Directions:

1. Blend brown sugar, granulated sugar, and butter in a mixing bowl using a hand or stand mixer for 2 minutes.
2. Pour in lemon juice, vanilla, and egg. Blend it on low speed for 30 seconds. Then mix on medium speed for 2–3 minutes until fluffy consistency.

3. Mix in on low-speed oats, flour, cinnamon, baking soda, and salt; blend for 45–60 seconds. Fold in walnuts and chocolate chips.

4. Preheat your air fryer to 300°F. Cover the inside of the air fryer basket with a piece of parchment paper.

5. Take about 2 tablespoons of the dough and shape a ball. Put in the preheated air fryer basket around 1½ to 2 inches apart. Flatten the tops of the cookies with wet hands.

6. Cook at 300°F for 6–8 minutes. Remove and cool for about 5 minutes before taking the cookies out, otherwise, they can crumble.

7. Repeat the last 2 steps with the remaining cookies.

8. Serve and enjoy your Chocolate Chip Cookies!

Nutrition:

Calories: 353 Carbohydrates: 39 g Fat: 20.1 g Protein: 5.4 g Sugar: 24.3 g Cholesterol: 43 mg

Gluten-Free Chocolate Cake

Preparation Time: 10 minutes

Cooking Time: 1 hour 15 minutes

Servings: 10

Ingredients:

- 1 cup of almond flour
- 2/3 cup of sugar
- 3 large eggs
- 1/3 cup of heavy cream
- ¼ cup of unsweetened cocoa powder
- ¼ cup of melted coconut oil
- ⅛ cup of chopped pecans
- ⅛ cup of chopped walnuts
- 1 tsp. of baking powder
- ½ tsp. of orange zest
- Unsalted butter, for greasing

Directions:

1. Take a 7-inch round baking pan, cover the bottom with parchment paper and grease it with unsalted butter.
2. Put all the ingredients into a large mixing bowl. Blend the mixture on medium speed using a hand mixer until you receive the fluffy and light batter.
3. Gently fold in the walnuts and pecans. Transfer the prepared batter into the baking pan and cover it with a piece of aluminum foil.

4. Put the baking pan into the air fryer basket. Cook at 325°F for 45 minutes. Take the foil out and cook for extra 10–15 minutes until done. To check the readiness, insert the toothpick in the center; it should come out clean.

5. Remove the pan from the air fryer. Let it cool for 10 minutes. Then take the cooked cake out from the pan and allow it to cool for extra 20 minutes.

6. Serve with berries and enjoy your Gluten-Free Chocolate Cake!

Nutrition: Calories: 232 Carbohydrates: 17 g Fat: 17 g Protein: 4 g Sugar: 13 g Sodium: 22 mg Cholesterol: 59 mg

Measurement Conversion Chart

- The charts you are seeing below will help you to convert the difference between units of volume in US customary units.
- Please note that US volume is not the same as in the UK and other countries, and many of the measurements are different depending on your country
- It's very easy to get confused when dealing with US and UK units! The good thing is that the metric units never change!
- All the measurement charts below are for US customary units only!
- We have gone to great length in order to make sure that the measurements on the following Measurement Charts are accurate.

Weight (Mass)

American Standard (Ounces)	Metric (Grams)
1/2 ounce	15 grams
1 ounce	30 grams
3 ounces	85 grams
3.75 ounces	100 grams
4 ounces	115 grams
8 ounces	225 grams
12 ounces	340 grams
16 ounces or 1 pound	450 grams

Oven Temperatures

American Standard	Metric
250° F	130° C
300° F	150° C
350° F	180° C
400° F	200° C
450° F	230° C

American and British Variances					
Term	Abbreviation	Nationality	Dry or liquid	Metric equivalent	Equivalent in context
cup	c., C.		usually liquid	237 milliliters	16 tablespoons or 8 ounces
ounce	fl oz, fl. oz.	American	liquid only	29.57 milliliters	
		British	either	28.41 milliliters	
gallon	gal.	American	liquid only	3.785 liters	4 quarts
		British	either	4.546 liters	4 quarts
inch	in, in.			2.54 centimeters	
ounce	oz, oz.	American	dry liquid	28.35 grams see OUNCE	1/16 pound see OUNCE
pint	p., pt.	American	liquid	0.473 liter	1/8 gallon or 16 ounces
			dry	0.551 liter	1/2 quart
		British	either	0.568 liter	
pound	lb.		dry	453.592 grams	16 ounces
Quart	q., qt, qt.	American	liquid	0.946 liter	1/4 gallon or 32 ounces
			dry	1.101 liters	2 pints
		British	either	1.136 liters	
Teaspoon	t., tsp., tsp		either	about 5 milliliters	1/3 tablespoon
Tablespoon	T., tbs., tbsp.		either	about 15 milliliters	3 teaspoons or 1/2 ounce

Volume (Dry)

American Standard	Metric
1/8 teaspoon	5 ml
1/4 teaspoon	1 ml
1/2 teaspoon	2 ml
3/4 teaspoon	4 ml
1 teaspoon	5 ml
1 tablespoon	15 ml
1/4 cup	59 ml
1/3 cup	79 ml
1/2 cup	118 ml
2/3 cup	158 ml
3/4 cup	177 ml
1 cup	225 ml
2 cups or 1 pint	450 ml
3 cups	675 ml
4 cups or 1 quart	1 liter
1/2 gallon	2 liters
1 gallon	4 liters

Dry Measure Equivalents

3 teaspoons	1 tablespoon	1/2 ounce	14.3 grams
2 tablespoons	1/8 cup	1 ounce	28.3 grams
4 tablespoons	1/4 cup	2 ounces	56.7 grams
5 1/3 tablespoons	1/3 cup	2.6 ounces	75.6 grams
8 tablespoons	1/2 cup	4 ounces	113.4 grams
12 tablespoons	3/4 cup	6 ounces	.375 pound
32 tablespoons	2 cups	16 ounces	1 pound

Volume (Liquid)

American Standard (Cups & Quarts)	American Standard (Ounces)	Metric (Milliliters & Liters)
2 tbsp.	1 fl. oz.	30 ml
1/4 cup	2 fl. oz.	60 ml
1/2 cup	4 fl. oz.	125 ml
1 cup	8 fl. oz.	250 ml
1 1/2 cups	12 fl. oz.	375 ml
2 cups or 1 pint	16 fl. oz.	500 ml
4 cups or 1 quart	32 fl. oz.	1000 ml or 1 liter
1 gallon	128 fl. oz.	4 liters

Conclusion

An air fryer is a smart appliance that can be used to cook food of various kinds. It can also be used to cook the food in an oven with little oil or butter. It uses air pressure to cook the food and fries it in your air fryer oven. With this, you will be able to cook healthier dishes without the burden of low temperatures that is required in the traditional oven cooking. This can save time and money because you are not using a conventional oven!

With the use of an air fryer, you can prepare your desired food without having to use any kind of oil or grease. The food gets fried in a healthier way without altering its taste or texture. The air fryer is available in many different sizes and several kinds of colors. Nowadays, many people prefer to use air fryers for preparing their daily meals because they are cheap and less messy than using traditional Directions of cooking.

You can control how much time your food will spend in the hot air fryer with its timer feature. This feature ensures that your foods are ready at the exact time you want them to be served. No need to worry about overcooking your foods because you have full control over how long they will be cooked with this unit. The air fryer is also known for keeping food at an ideal temperature. This means if you want to achieve a crispy crust on your chicken, you need to make sure that the air fryer is set at the right temperature.

If done properly, it will be able to cook food without affecting its taste or texture. You will never have to worry about your food getting burnt because it will be cooked at a proper temperature. Another advantage of using an air fryer is that it reduces the amount of oil used in cooking. It allows you to cook many foods without having to use oil or butter. The food only needs to be coated with the oil that is used. It will work as an excellent healthier method of cooking. You can prepare your food in no time at all and eat it on the same day.

An air fryer is also known for being heat resistant, thus, it does not need to be cleaned or serviced often. This can make it more convenient for you since you will not have to hire a professional to clean and service this appliance for you.

The air fryer oven has many features that enable you to prepare tasty foods easily and efficiently. I hope this cookbook helps you find new ways to prepare your favorite dishes.

CPSIA information can be obtained
at www.ICGtesting.com
Printed in the USA
LVHW081606120621
690059LV00002B/181